Spotter's Guide for
COUNTRY WALKS

Karen Goaman

Contents

Most of the illustrations in this book have been previously published in the Usborne *Spotter's Guide* series.

Designed by Anne Sharples

Special Consultant
Keith Kirby

Illustrators
Joyce Bee, Trevor Boyer, Hilary Burn, Victoria Goaman, Ian Jackson, Annabel Milne, Chris Shields, Peter Stebbing, Phil Weare.

First published in 1982 by
Usborne Publishing Limited,
Usborne House, 83-85 Saffron Hill,
London EC1N 8RT

Printed in Great Britain

The name Usborne and the device 🐝 are Trade Marks of Usborne Publishing Ltd.

Red Squirrel

How to use this book

This book will help you to identify many of the very common plants and animals which you are likely to see on a country walk.

The description next to each illustration tells you where each species (type of plant or animal) grows or lives. If there are any words you do not understand, look them up in the glossary.

There is a small circle beside each description. Whenever you see and identify a species, put a tick in the appropriate circle.

There is a **scorecard** at the end of the book. This awards you a score for each plant or animal that you spot. A very common one scores 5 points, a less common one 10 points. Add up your score after a country walk, and see how many points you can get each time.

Birds

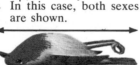

In some species, the male (♂) and female (♀) are very different. In this case, both sexes are shown.

The length of each bird, from beak to tip of tail, is given in centimetres.

Mammals

The body length is given in centimetres. This is the length of head and body but excluding the tail.

Butterflies and moths

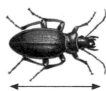

The wingspan is given in millimetres.

Other insects

The body length, excluding legs and antennae, is given in millimetres.

Wild flowers, fern, grasses

For some flowers extra close-up pictures of the flower or fruit are shown.

The height from ground level to the top of the plant is given in centimetres or metres.

Fungi

Never taste or eat any fungi since many species are poisonous.

For mushrooms and toadstools the width of the cap is given in centimetres.

Trees

The illustrations show the whole tree in summer and, if it is deciduous (loses its leaves each autumn), the bare tree in winter. They also show close-ups of the bark and leaves.

Height shown in metres

Looking at the countryside

Once you are able to identify some species of wildlife, walks in the country become even more interesting and fun. Notice too the type of countryside around you. You may find yourself walking through many different habitats, such as those described below.

Woodland. Broadleaved woods may be rich in wildlife, but conifer plantations are dark and few plants and animals live in them.

Hedgerows. These are hedges of trees and shrubs planted to mark boundaries between fields or along roadsides. They are a rich wildlife habitat, being a mixture of woodland and open grassland.

Grassland. Occurs on downs, in old meadows and even in places such as churchyards. Provided it is not mown too often or grazed too heavily it will be rich in flowers and insects.

Heathland. This occurs on poor, sandy soils in lowland areas. Typical heathland plants are heather, bracken and gorse. Birch and Scots pine trees may also be found growing on heaths.

Moorland. This is similar to heathland but is found on upland areas. The plants found on heaths are often found on moors, but moorland has larger areas of coarse grasses.

◄ Mute Swan

Seen all year on rivers and lakes. Normally it is silent, but if irritated hisses or gives a snorting grunt. Young are called cygnets. 152 cm.

Its long neck helps it feed under water

Cygnet

Mallard ►

Found on all kinds of still and slow-moving water. Wild Mallard often cross-breed with domestic farm ducks. Only the duck (female) gives the familiar "quack". 58 cm.

♀

♂

♀

Tuft

♂

◄ Tufted Duck

Seen on ponds, lakes and reservoirs. More common in winter. Dives for food and can swim underwater. Drake has long tuft, duck has shorter one. 43 cm.

5

BIRDS

Black crest

Has long legs which trail out in flight

◀ Grey Heron

Usually seen near freshwater and estuaries. Feeds, often from the water, on fish, frogs and small mammals. Nests in trees. 92 cm.

Coot ▶

Usually seen on lakes and reservoirs rather than small ponds. Adult birds have white "shield" on forehead. Dives to feed on water plants. 38 cm.

◀ Moorhen

Lives on any small area of water, preferring water surrounded by thick vegetation. Feeds on land and water. 33 cm.

Red bill with yellow tip

Black-headed Gull ▶

Common inland and near the sea. Has dark brown head in summer only; in winter head turns white with brown smudge. 38 cm.

Winter

Summer

Long pointed wings

♀

♂

Long tail

Very long tail

♂

Cocks often have a white neck ring

♀

Broad, rounded wings

◀ Kestrel

Can be seen in open countryside. Hovers when hunting. Sometimes seen hovering alongside motorways, looking for prey. Eats birds, mammals, and insects. 34 cm.

▲ Pheasant

Lives on farmland with hedges and woods. Often reared and shot as game. Nests on ground. Cocks vary in colour.
Male 87 cm.
Female 58 cm.

◀ Lapwing

Seen on farmland, estuaries and mudflats. Forms large flocks in winter. Looks black and white at a distance. Its call is a "pee-wit".
30 cm.

Woodpigeon ▶

A common bird of farmland, woods and towns. Forms large flocks in winter. Its call is a familiar "coo-coo-coo, coo-coo". 41 cm.

White on wings

White on tail

◀ Collared Dove

Often found around farm buildings, and in gardens and parks. Feeds mainly on grain. Sometimes seen in flocks. 30 cm.

Great Spotted Woodpecker ▶

Lives in woods, nesting in tree holes. Drums on trees in spring. Has a bouncing flight. 23 cm.

Large white patches on wings

Pied Wagtail ▶

Seen mainly on farmland and near freshwater. Also found in towns. Tends to run rather than walk. 18 cm.

Wags its tail up and down

Swift ▶

A summer visitor, found in Britain from May to August. Flies fast over country and towns in flocks. Listen for its screaming call. 17 cm.

Swift's tail is forked

All dark underneath apart from whitish throat

Swallow's tail has streamers

White underparts

Chestnut throat

◀ Swallow

Summer visitor to Britain, found from April to October. Often seen near freshwater. Catches insects in flight. Nests in buildings. 19 cm.

Dunnock ▶

Lives in all kinds of bushy places, woods, parks and gardens. Looks a bit like a female House Sparrow (p. 10), but note grey head. 14 cm.

Often cocks its tail up

Very small bird

◀ Wren

Found in all kinds of places including woods, heaths, parks and gardens. Loud song finishes with a trill. Never keeps still for long. 9.5 cm.

◀ **House Sparrow**

Very common bird. Lives near houses, and even in city centres. Often seen in flocks. Has a chirping song. 15 cm.

Robin ▶

A woodland bird, also common in gardens. Has a warbling song, and a "tic, tic" call when alarmed. Male and female look alike. 14 cm.

Red face and breast

◀ **Starling**

Very common bird, found on farmland, in woody places, parks and towns. Often roosts in huge flocks. Mimics songs of other birds. 22 cm.

Blackbird ▶

Lives where there are trees and bushes, often in parks and gardens. Some Blackbirds have patches of white feathers. 25 cm.

Song Thrush ▶

Found in or near trees and bushes. Well-known for the way it breaks open snail shells. Often seen in gardens. 23 cm.

◀ Coal Tit

Most common in conifer woods, but also seen in broadleaved trees, and gardens. Has white patch on back of head. 11 cm.

Great Tit ▶

Lives in woodlands, heaths and gardens. Nests in holes in trees. The largest tit. Note its black and white head. 14 cm.

Black band on belly

Thin dark line on belly

◀ Blue Tit

Seen in woods, hedgerows and gardens. Look for the bright blue on top of its head. 11 cm.

♀

♂

◄ Bullfinch
Often found on the edges of woods, in hedges and in gardens. Eats seeds. Its white rump shows in flight. 15 cm.

♀

♂

Chaffinch ►
Likely to be found wherever there are trees and bushes, including in gardens. Often flocks with other finches in winter. 15 cm.

◄ Goldfinch
Feeds on thistle seeds and other weed seeds in open places. Look for its red face and yellow on wings. 12 cm.

Greenfinch ►
Seen on woodland edges. Also on farmland and in gardens, especially in winter. A yellow-green bird. 12 cm.

♀

♂

Rook ▶

Nests communally in "rookeries" in tops of trees. Is usually seen in flocks on farmland. Voice is a harsh "kaw". 46 cm.

Young birds lack bare skin around beak

Baggy thigh feathers

◀ Magpie

Seen amongst trees, on farmland and in towns. Eats eggs and young of other kinds of birds in spring. 46 cm.

◀ Jay

A secretive bird of woody areas and large gardens. Listen for its screeching call. 32 cm.

Carrion Crow ▶

Common bird, found in all types of country. Has a rather heavy flight. 47 cm.

13

Bushy tail

Red Fox ▶

Lives on farmland and in woods. Feeds mainly by night catching small mammals, birds, poultry.
Body length 65 cm.

◀ Grey Squirrel

Common in woods, parks and gardens. Its coat may have patches of brown. The much rarer Red Squirrel lives mainly in northern woods.
Body length 27 cm.

Rabbit ▶

Common on farmland and hillsides. Large groups live together in burrows underground. Feeds on plants. Active dusk and dawn.
Body length 40 cm.

Prickles

◀ Hedgehog

Seen in hedgerows, woods, ditches, parks and gardens. Active mainly at night. Snuffles, squeals and snores. Rolls into a ball when alarmed.
Body length 25 cm.

Fallow Deer ▶

Lives in herds in parks and woods. Only male has antlers and loses these after the mating season (the "rut") in October. Height to shoulder 1 m.

Roe Deer ▶

Lives in conifer wood plantations, near water. Red-brown in summer, grey-brown in winter. Only male has antlers; loses these after summer "rut". Height to shoulder 70 cm.

White spots on coat ♂

♂

◀ Common Shrew

Seen in woods, hedgerows, dunes and marshes. Has a very high shrill squeak. Body length 7 cm.

Field Vole ▶

Quite common on open ground. Rarely climbs, but makes tunnels through the undergrowth. Body length 11 cm.

Quite shaggy hair

Has short tail

◀ Wood Mouse

Found in hedgerows, woods and gardens. Digs burrows. Climbs and moves fast, making long leaps. Body length 9 cm.

Has large ears

Long "ringed" tail

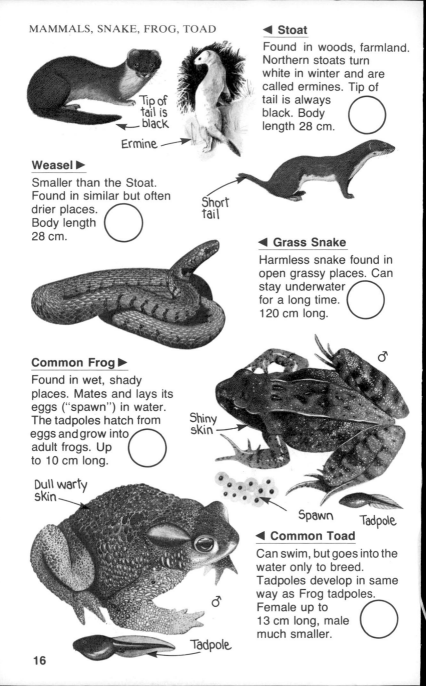

◀ Stoat

Found in woods, farmland. Northern stoats turn white in winter and are called ermines. Tip of tail is always black. Body length 28 cm.

Tip of tail is black

Ermine →

Weasel ▶

Smaller than the Stoat. Found in similar but often drier places. Body length 28 cm.

Short tail

◀ Grass Snake

Harmless snake found in open grassy places. Can stay underwater for a long time. 120 cm long.

Common Frog ▶

Found in wet, shady places. Mates and lays its eggs ("spawn") in water. The tadpoles hatch from eggs and grow into adult frogs. Up to 10 cm long.

Shiny skin →

♂

Dull warty skin →

Spawn

Tadpole

◀ Common Toad

Can swim, but goes into the water only to breed. Tadpoles develop in same way as Frog tadpoles. Female up to 13 cm long, male much smaller.

♂

Tadpole

♂

Female
is paler
and
duller

◀ Brimstone

Seen in hedges and along woodland paths. Caterpillar feeds on buckthorn plants. Wingspan 59 mm.

Small Tortoiseshell ▶

Visits all kinds of flowers. Quite common all over Britain. Seen from April to November. Wingspan 50 mm.

Meadow Brown ▼

Seen in meadows and grassy places where it visits thistles, knapweed and bramble flowers. Wingspan 50–55 mm.

♂

♀

Small Heath ▶

Found in all kinds of countryside – open woods, marshes and dry hillsides. Likes hawkweed flowers. Wingspan 34 mm.

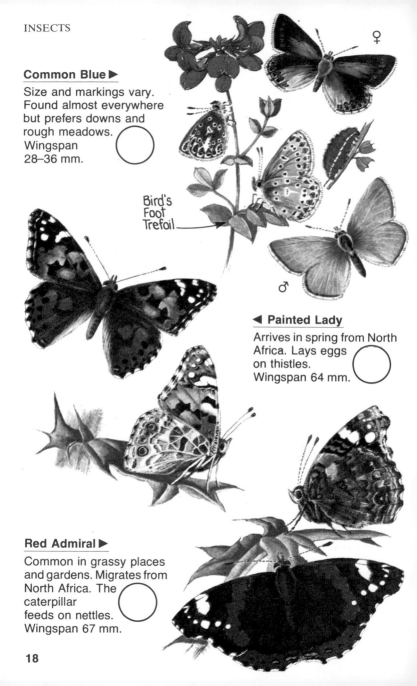

Common Blue ▶

Size and markings vary.
Found almost everywhere
but prefers downs and
rough meadows.
Wingspan
28–36 mm.

Bird's
Foot
Trefoil —

♀

♂

◀ Painted Lady

Arrives in spring from North
Africa. Lays eggs
on thistles.
Wingspan 64 mm.

Red Admiral ▶

Common in grassy places
and gardens. Migrates from
North Africa. The
caterpillar
feeds on nettles.
Wingspan 67 mm.

Peacock ▶

Common in open fields, woodland and in gardens. The caterpillar feeds on nettles. Butterflies seen April to September. Wingspan 65 mm.

The markings are like the "eyes" on a peacock's tail

Cabbage leaf

♀

♂

Large White ▶

Found in woods, open country and gardens. Caterpillar eats cabbage plants. Butterflies seen from April to October. Wingspan 63 mm.

♀

19

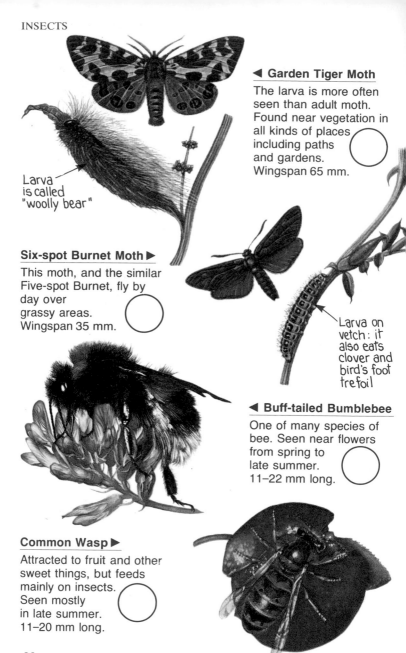

◄ Garden Tiger Moth

The larva is more often seen than adult moth. Found near vegetation in all kinds of places including paths and gardens. Wingspan 65 mm.

Larva is called "woolly bear"

Six-spot Burnet Moth ►

This moth, and the similar Five-spot Burnet, fly by day over grassy areas. Wingspan 35 mm.

Larva on vetch: it also eats clover and bird's foot trefoil

◄ Buff-tailed Bumblebee

One of many species of bee. Seen near flowers from spring to late summer. 11–22 mm long.

Common Wasp ►

Attracted to fruit and other sweet things, but feeds mainly on insects. Seen mostly in late summer. 11–20 mm long.

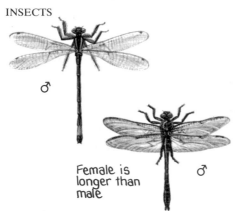

♂

Female is longer than male

♂

◄ Blue-tailed Damselfly

Seen on plants near still or slow-moving water in summer.
Wingspan 35 mm.
30 mm long.

◄ Golden-ringed Dragonfly

Near streams and rivers, but like many dragonflies it is sometimes seen far from water. Wingspan 100 mm.
75–85 mm long.

Seven-spot Ladybird ►

As common as the Two-spot Ladybird. Both are found in all kinds of places with vegetation.
6–7 mm long.

◄ Violet Ground Beetle

Common in woods, under hedges and in gardens. Eats other insects and worms.
30–35 mm. long.

Red Ant ►

Nests under stones or in rotting wood. Like the Black Ant (not shown), is very common. Like all ants, males and queens grow wings for the mating flight.
3–6 mm long.

Nest in tree stump

Long antennae

◀ Speckled Bush Cricket

Seen in late summer or early autumn in shrubby places. Bush crickets have long antennae, grasshoppers have short antennae. ◯
46 mm long.

Common Earwig ▶

Eats small, usually dead, insects, as well as ◯ leaves and fruits.
15 mm long.

◀ Garden Spider

Spins a web to catch flies and other insects. Female is much larger than male. Not an insect but an "arachnid", ◯ having eight legs.
7–18 mm long.

Garden Snail ▶

Found everywhere, on long grass or on old walls. Hides under stones in daytime, feeds on ◯ plants at night.

Shell is 25 – 35 mm across

Snail is a "mollusc", not an insect

Larva

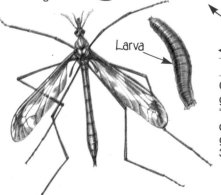

◀ Daddy Long Legs or Giant Cranefly

Often near water or in gardens. Larvae (called "leatherjackets") eat root crops and grass roots. ◯
30–40 mm long.

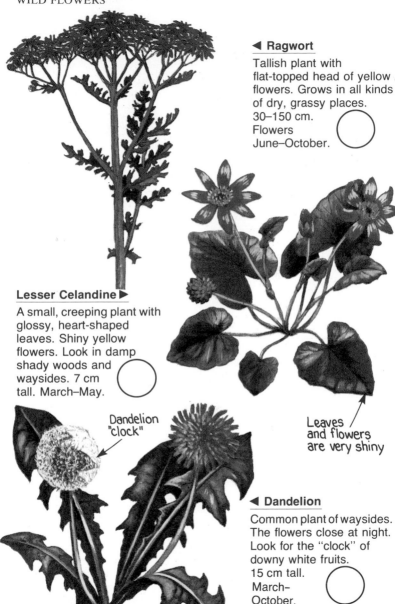

◄ Ragwort

Tallish plant with
flat-topped head of yellow
flowers. Grows in all kinds
of dry, grassy places.
30–150 cm.
Flowers
June–October.

Lesser Celandine ►

A small, creeping plant with
glossy, heart-shaped
leaves. Shiny yellow
flowers. Look in damp
shady woods and
waysides. 7 cm
tall. March–May.

Dandelion
"clock"

Leaves
and flowers
are very shiny

◄ Dandelion

Common plant of waysides.
The flowers close at night.
Look for the "clock" of
downy white fruits.
15 cm tall.
March–
October.

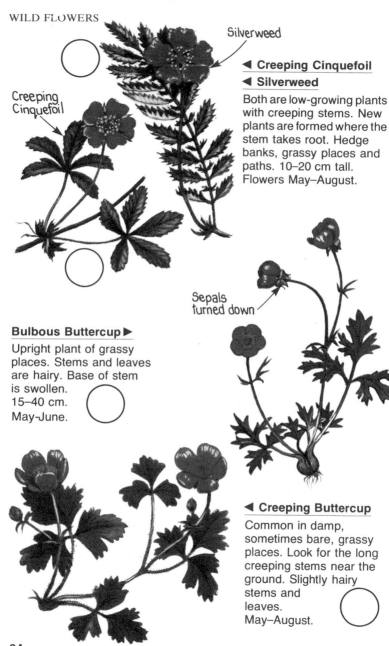

Silverweed

◀ Creeping Cinquefoil
◀ Silverweed

Both are low-growing plants with creeping stems. New plants are formed where the stem takes root. Hedge banks, grassy places and paths. 10–20 cm tall. Flowers May–August.

Creeping Cinquefoil

Sepals turned down

Bulbous Buttercup ▶

Upright plant of grassy places. Stems and leaves are hairy. Base of stem is swollen. 15–40 cm. May-June.

◀ Creeping Buttercup

Common in damp, sometimes bare, grassy places. Look for the long creeping stems near the ground. Slightly hairy stems and leaves. May–August.

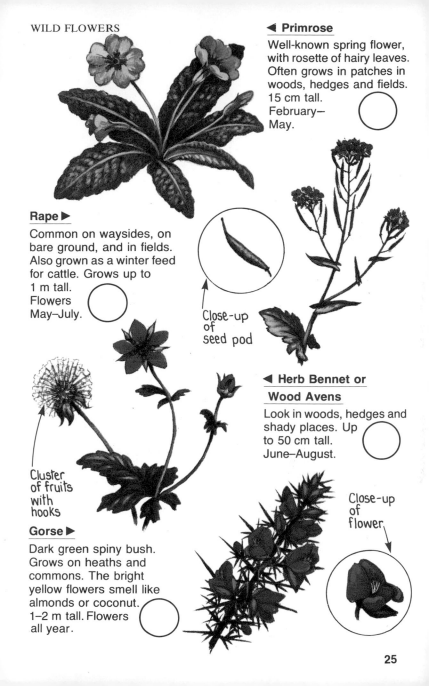

◀ Primrose

Well-known spring flower, with rosette of hairy leaves. Often grows in patches in woods, hedges and fields. 15 cm tall. February–May.

Rape ▶

Common on waysides, on bare ground, and in fields. Also grown as a winter feed for cattle. Grows up to 1 m tall. Flowers May–July.

Close-up of seed pod

◀ Herb Bennet or Wood Avens

Look in woods, hedges and shady places. Up to 50 cm tall. June–August.

Cluster of fruits with hooks

Gorse ▶

Dark green spiny bush. Grows on heaths and commons. The bright yellow flowers smell like almonds or coconut. 1–2 m tall. Flowers all year.

Close-up of flower

25

The seed pods look like birds' claws

◄ Bird's Foot Trefoil

Look for this small creeping plant in grassy places and on downs. Also called "bacon and eggs" because flowers are streaked with red. May–July.

▼ Honeysuckle

Climbing plant seen in hedges and woods, with very fragrant flower. Fruits are berries which ripen to red in autumn. Up to 6 m. June–September.

◄ Groundsel

Found in fields and other cultivated places. Flowers all year. 8–45 cm tall.

Lady's Smock ▶

Grows in damp places such as meadows, and on roadsides especially near streams. Flowers can be pink, lilac or white.
15–60 cm tall.
April–June.

▼ Herb Robert

Spreading plant which grows in woods, hedgebanks, and in walls. Leaves are red in autumn.
40 cm tall.
May–September.

Close-up of fruit

Fluffy white seeds seen in autumn

Rosebay Willowherb ▶

Tall plant with spikes of pink flowers. Common on edges of woods, roadsides, and waste ground.
30–120 cm tall.
July–September.

27

The white flowers have purplish veins so they look pink

Wood Sorrel ▶

A creeping woodland plant with slender stems and rounded leaves. Grows in woods, hedges and shady places.
10 cm tall.
April–May

Ripe berry (can be eaten)

◀ Blackberry or Bramble

Dense woody plant that climbs up hedges. Grows in woods, along paths and lanes, and on waste ground. Flowers June–September.
Berries ripen in autumn.

Thorns

Dogrose ▶

Scrambling creeper, up to 3 m tall, with thorny stems. Look for the red fruits, called rose hips, in autumn. Hedges and woods. Flowers June–July.

Rose hip (fruit)

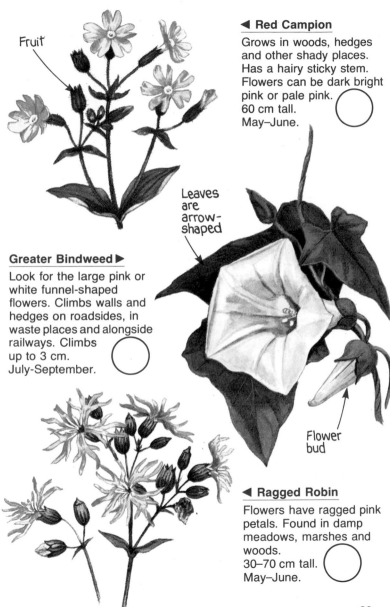

Fruit

◀ Red Campion

Grows in woods, hedges and other shady places. Has a hairy sticky stem. Flowers can be dark bright pink or pale pink.
60 cm tall.
May–June.

Leaves are arrow-shaped

Greater Bindweed ▶

Look for the large pink or white funnel-shaped flowers. Climbs walls and hedges on roadsides, in waste places and alongside railways. Climbs up to 3 cm.
July-September.

Flower bud

◀ Ragged Robin

Flowers have ragged pink petals. Found in damp meadows, marshes and woods.
30–70 cm tall.
May–June.

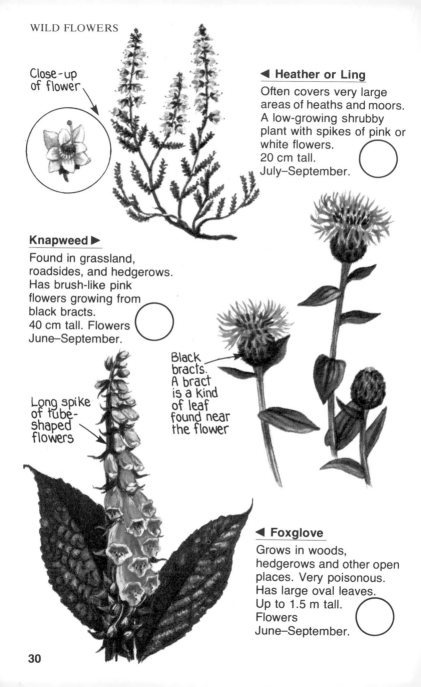

Close-up of flower

◄ Heather or Ling

Often covers very large areas of heaths and moors. A low-growing shrubby plant with spikes of pink or white flowers.
20 cm tall.
July–September.

Knapweed ►

Found in grassland, roadsides, and hedgerows. Has brush-like pink flowers growing from black bracts.
40 cm tall. Flowers June–September.

Black bracts. A bract is a kind of leaf found near the flower

Long spike of tube-shaped flowers

◄ Foxglove

Grows in woods, hedgerows and other open places. Very poisonous. Has large oval leaves.
Up to 1.5 m tall.
Flowers June–September.

Scarlet Pimpernel ▶

Grows along the ground, on cultivated land and roadsides. The flowers close at mid-afternoon and in bad weather.
15 cm tall.
June–August.

Flowers may also be blue

Seed pod

Flower bud

◀ Poppy

Grows on waste ground, roadsides and cornfields. The soft red flowers have dark centres. Stiff hairs on stem. Up to 60 cm tall.
June–August.

Close-up of flower

Wood Woundwort ▶

Strongly-smelling plant of hedges, woods and other shady places. The leaves were once used to dress wounds.
40 cm tall.
June–August.

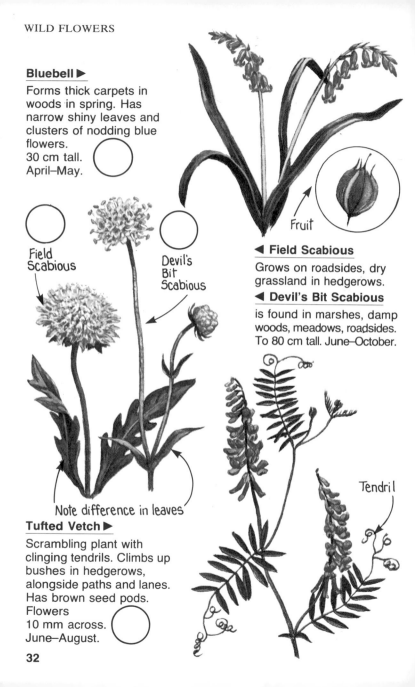

Bluebell ▶

Forms thick carpets in woods in spring. Has narrow shiny leaves and clusters of nodding blue flowers.
30 cm tall.
April–May.

Field Scabious

Devil's Bit Scabious

Fruit

◀ Field Scabious

Grows on roadsides, dry grassland in hedgerows.

◀ Devil's Bit Scabious

is found in marshes, damp woods, meadows, roadsides. To 80 cm tall. June–October.

Note difference in leaves

Tufted Vetch ▶

Scrambling plant with clinging tendrils. Climbs up bushes in hedgerows, alongside paths and lanes. Has brown seed pods.
Flowers
10 mm across.
June–August.

Tendril

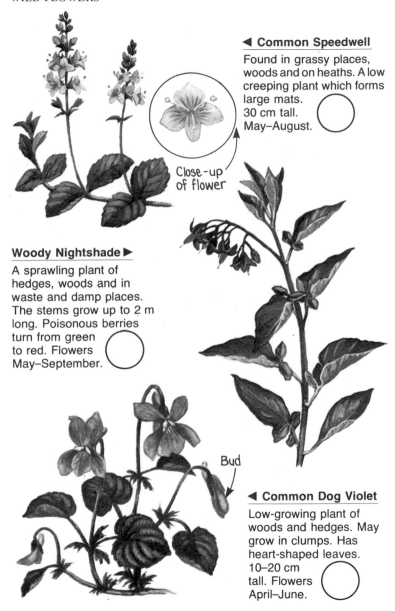

◀ Common Speedwell

Found in grassy places, woods and on heaths. A low creeping plant which forms large mats. 30 cm tall. May–August.

Close-up of flower

Woody Nightshade ▶

A sprawling plant of hedges, woods and in waste and damp places. The stems grow up to 2 m long. Poisonous berries turn from green to red. Flowers May–September.

Bud

◀ Common Dog Violet

Low-growing plant of woods and hedges. May grow in clumps. Has heart-shaped leaves. 10–20 cm tall. Flowers April–June.

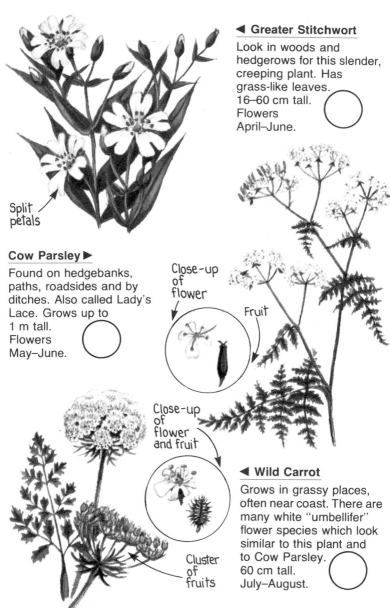

◀ Greater Stitchwort

Look in woods and hedgerows for this slender, creeping plant. Has grass-like leaves. 16–60 cm tall. Flowers April–June.

Split petals

Cow Parsley ▶

Found on hedgebanks, paths, roadsides and by ditches. Also called Lady's Lace. Grows up to 1 m tall. Flowers May–June.

Close-up of flower

Fruit

Close-up of flower and fruit

◀ Wild Carrot

Grows in grassy places, often near coast. There are many white "umbellifer" flower species which look similar to this plant and to Cow Parsley. 60 cm tall. July–August.

Cluster of fruits

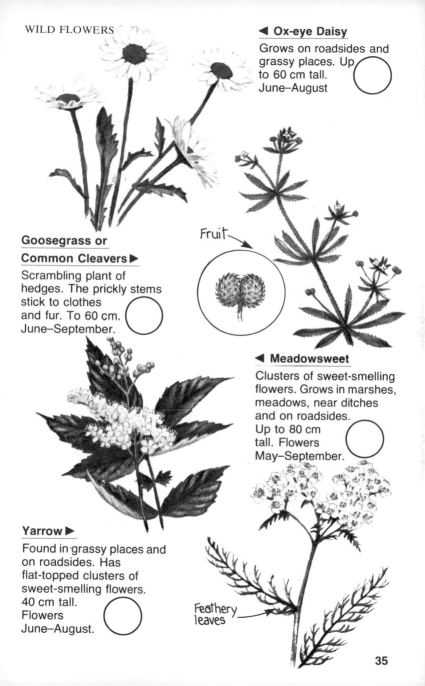

◀ Ox-eye Daisy

Grows on roadsides and grassy places. Up to 60 cm tall. June–August

Goosegrass or Common Cleavers ▶

Scrambling plant of hedges. The prickly stems stick to clothes and fur. To 60 cm. June–September.

Fruit

◀ Meadowsweet

Clusters of sweet-smelling flowers. Grows in marshes, meadows, near ditches and on roadsides. Up to 80 cm tall. Flowers May–September.

Yarrow ▶

Found in grassy places and on roadsides. Has flat-topped clusters of sweet-smelling flowers. 40 cm tall. Flowers June–August.

Feathery leaves

35

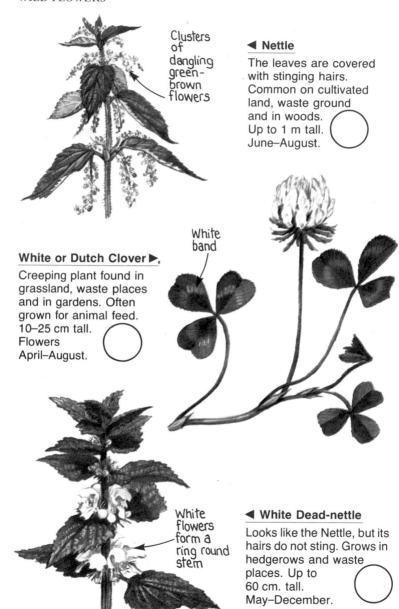

Clusters
of
dangling
green-
brown
flowers

◄ Nettle

The leaves are covered with stinging hairs. Common on cultivated land, waste ground and in woods. Up to 1 m tall. June–August.

White band

White or Dutch Clover ►

Creeping plant found in grassland, waste places and in gardens. Often grown for animal feed. 10–25 cm tall. Flowers April–August.

White flowers form a ring round stem

◄ White Dead-nettle

Looks like the Nettle, but its hairs do not sting. Grows in hedgerows and waste places. Up to 60 cm. tall. May–December.

Jack-by-the Hedge or Garlic Mustard ▶

Grows in hedges and open woods. Smells of garlic. Up to 1.2 m tall. Flowers April–June.

Seed pods

Yellow anthers

◀ Black Nightshade

Shrubby plant of cultivated ground. Petals fold back to show yellow anthers. Poisonous berries turn from green to black. 20 cm tall. July–September.

White petals sometimes tinged with pink

Daisy ▶

Grows in short grass and is very common in garden lawns. The flowers close at night and in bad weather. Up to 10 cm tall. Flowers March–October.

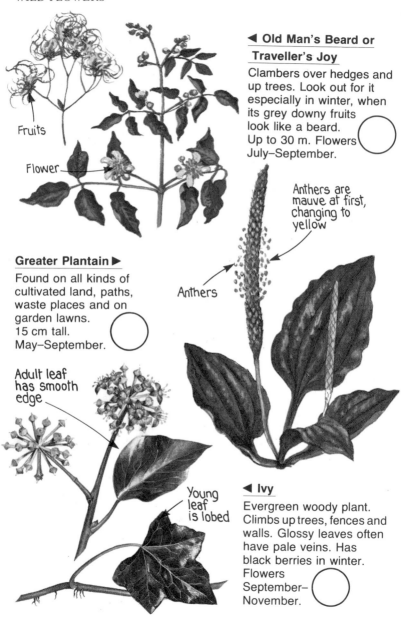

◄ Old Man's Beard or Traveller's Joy

Clambers over hedges and up trees. Look out for it especially in winter, when its grey downy fruits look like a beard. Up to 30 m. Flowers July–September.

Fruits

Flower

Anthers are mauve at first, changing to yellow

Anthers

Greater Plantain ►

Found on all kinds of cultivated land, paths, waste places and on garden lawns. 15 cm tall. May–September.

Adult leaf has smooth edge

Young leaf is lobed

◄ Ivy

Evergreen woody plant. Climbs up trees, fences and walls. Glossy leaves often have pale veins. Has black berries in winter. Flowers September–November.

38

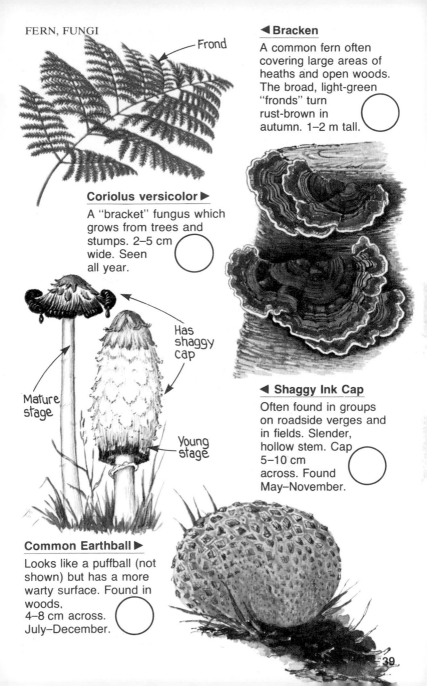

Frond

◀ Bracken

A common fern often covering large areas of heaths and open woods. The broad, light-green "fronds" turn rust-brown in autumn. 1–2 m tall.

Coriolus versicolor ▶

A "bracket" fungus which grows from trees and stumps. 2–5 cm wide. Seen all year.

Has shaggy cap

Mature stage

Young stage

◀ Shaggy Ink Cap

Often found in groups on roadside verges and in fields. Slender, hollow stem. Cap 5–10 cm across. Found May–November.

Common Earthball ▶

Looks like a puffball (not shown) but has a more warty surface. Found in woods. 4–8 cm across. July–December.

Fly Agaric ▶

Grows under birch and pine trees, often on sandy soil. Poisonous.
Cap 6–12 cm.
August–November.

Mature stage with orange-red cap

Young stage with bright-red cap

Mature stage

Young stage

Ring

Snake-like bands on stem

◀ Parasol

Found in woods and grassy places. Stem has snake-like patterns and is swollen at base.
Cap 5–15 cm.
July–November.

Yellow-green underneath cap

Sulphur Tuft ▶

Grows in clusters on broadleaved tree stumps, often in large numbers. Faint ring on stem.
Cap 4–10 cm.
August–November.

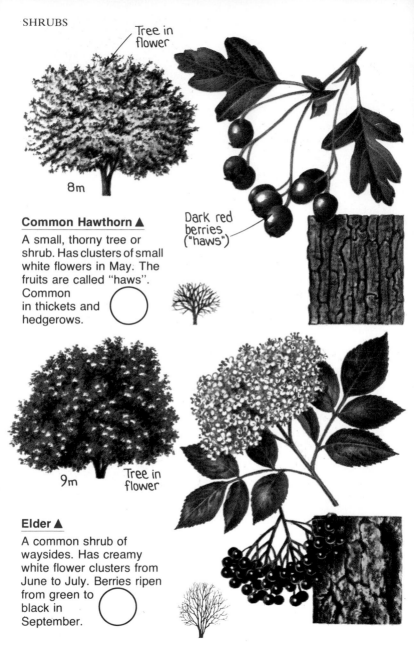

Tree in flower

8m

Common Hawthorn ▲

A small, thorny tree or shrub. Has clusters of small white flowers in May: The fruits are called "haws". Common in thickets and hedgerows.

Dark red berries ("haws")

9m Tree in flower

Elder ▲

A common shrub of waysides. Has creamy white flower clusters from June to July. Berries ripen from green to black in September.

41

Bigger lobes than Sessile Oak leaf

Acorn cup

Lobe

23m

Long stalk

English Oak ▲

The tree is often wider than it is high. Has a stout trunk with many large, twisted branches growing from the same point.

21m

Sessile Oak ▲

A narrower tree with a longer trunk than the English Oak (above). Its branches grow from different levels and tend to point upwards.

Acorns are often stalkless

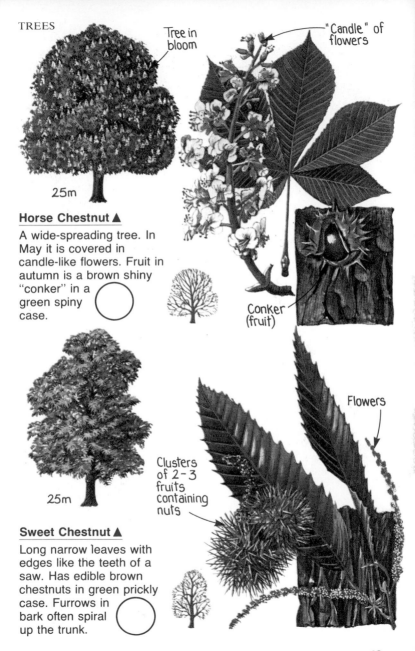

Tree in bloom

"Candle" of flowers

25m

Horse Chestnut ▲

A wide-spreading tree. In May it is covered in candle-like flowers. Fruit in autumn is a brown shiny "conker" in a green spiny case.

Conker (fruit)

Flowers

Clusters of 2–3 fruits containing nuts

25m

Sweet Chestnut ▲

Long narrow leaves with edges like the teeth of a saw. Has edible brown chestnuts in green prickly case. Furrows in bark often spiral up the trunk.

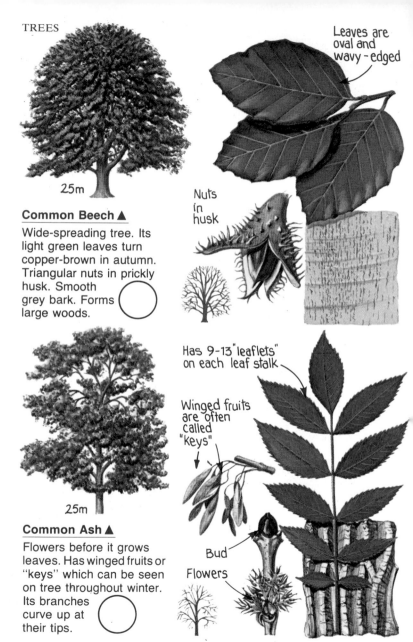

Leaves are oval and wavy-edged

25m

Common Beech ▲

Wide-spreading tree. Its light green leaves turn copper-brown in autumn. Triangular nuts in prickly husk. Smooth grey bark. Forms large woods.

Nuts in husk

Has 9-13 "leaflets" on each leaf stalk

Winged fruits are often called "keys"

25m

Common Ash ▲

Flowers before it grows leaves. Has winged fruits or "keys" which can be seen on tree throughout winter. Its branches curve up at their tips.

Bud

Flowers

44

20m

White Willow ▲

Like all willows, leaves are much paler underneath. Common by streams and rivers, and in wet woods and marshes. Catkins appear in April.

Underside of leaf

Long, narrow leaves

Catkin

15m

Silver Birch ▲

Grows in woods and on heathland. A slender tree with branches drooping at the tips. The catkins or "lamb's tails" open in April.

Pointed tip to leaves

Catkin, sometimes called "lamb's tail"

Silvery bark peels off in ribbons

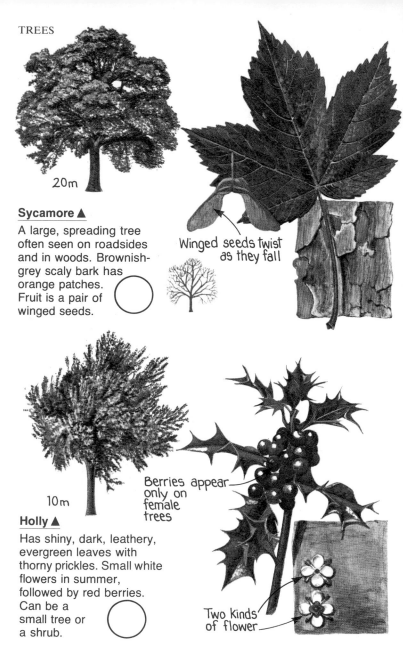

Sycamore ▲

A large, spreading tree often seen on roadsides and in woods. Brownish-grey scaly bark has orange patches. Fruit is a pair of winged seeds.

Winged seeds twist as they fall

Berries appear only on female trees

Holly ▲

Has shiny, dark, leathery, evergreen leaves with thorny prickles. Small white flowers in summer, followed by red berries. Can be a small tree or a shrub.

Two kinds of flower

20m

10m

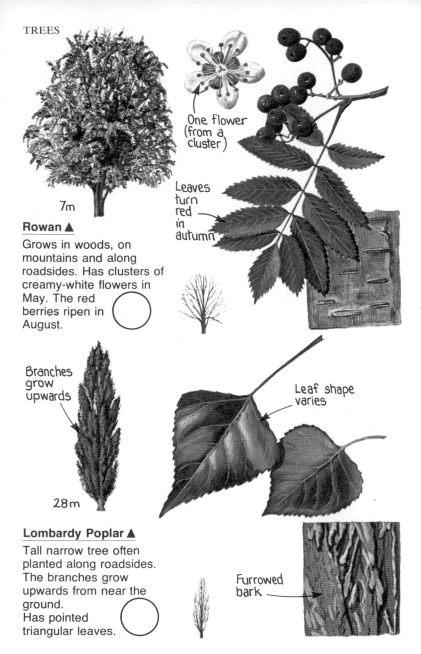

One flower
(from a
cluster)

Leaves
turn
red
in
autumn

7m

Rowan ▲

Grows in woods, on
mountains and along
roadsides. Has clusters of
creamy-white flowers in
May. The red
berries ripen in
August.

Branches
grow
upwards

Leaf shape
varies

28m

Lombardy Poplar ▲

Tall narrow tree often
planted along roadsides.
The branches grow
upwards from near the
ground.
Has pointed
triangular leaves.

Furrowed
bark

47

40m

Douglas Fir ▲

Seen in forestry plantations and large gardens. A tall conifer. The lowest branches often bend almost to touch ground. Light brown hanging cones.

Cone has 3-pointed bracts

Bracts

35m

Scots Pine ▲

Seen in woods on sandy soils and in plantations. Has blue-green needles in pairs. Pointed cone. Mature trees have a long bare trunk with red bark near top.

Long, bare trunk is red near top of tree

Short, paired needles

Bark flakes off in places

48

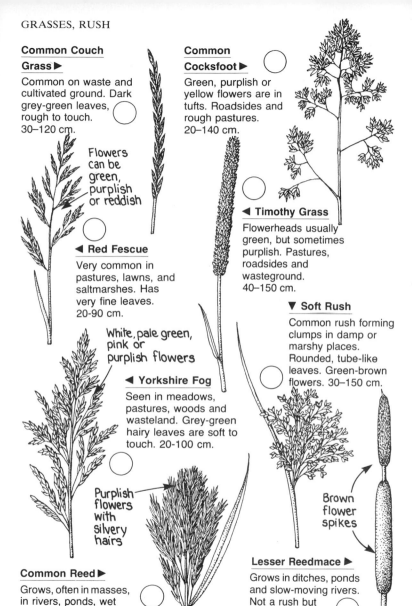

Common Couch Grass ▶

Common on waste and cultivated ground. Dark grey-green leaves, rough to touch. 30–120 cm.

Flowers can be green, purplish or reddish

◀ Red Fescue

Very common in pastures, lawns, and saltmarshes. Has very fine leaves. 20-90 cm.

White, pale green, pink or purplish flowers

◀ Yorkshire Fog

Seen in meadows, pastures, woods and wasteland. Grey-green hairy leaves are soft to touch. 20-100 cm.

Purplish flowers with silvery hairs

Common Reed ▶

Grows, often in masses, in rivers, ponds, wet meadows. Used for thatching roofs. Up to 3 m.

Common Cocksfoot ▶

Green, purplish or yellow flowers are in tufts. Roadsides and rough pastures. 20–140 cm.

◀ Timothy Grass

Flowerheads usually green, but sometimes purplish. Pastures, roadsides and wasteground. 40–150 cm.

▼ Soft Rush

Common rush forming clumps in damp or marshy places. Rounded, tube-like leaves. Green-brown flowers. 30–150 cm.

Brown flower spikes

Lesser Reedmace ▶

Grows in ditches, ponds and slow-moving rivers. Not a rush but sometimes called 'bulrush'. 1–3 m.

49

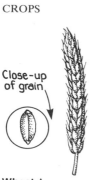

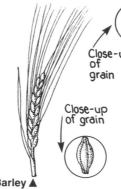

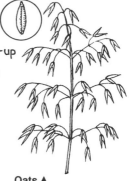

Close-up of grain

Close-up of grain

Close-up of grain

Wheat ▲

Grown on fertile soil. Used mainly for making bread, and for feeding farm animals. Sown mainly in autumn, some in spring.

Barley ▲

The most widespread cereal crop in Britain. Grown mainly for feeding farm animals. Some is used for beer.

Oats ▲

Grows on poorish soil, does not need much sun. Seen more in north. Mainly used for feeding livestock but some used for porridge etc.

Black Mustard (leaf)

Oil-seed rape

◀ Mustard and Oil-seed Rape

Both have yellow flowers and create fields of bright yellow in summer. Oil-seed Rape is grown for oil and cattle feed and Mustard for making table mustard.

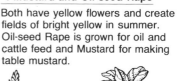

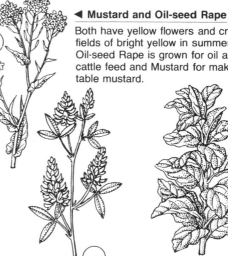

Sugar Beet ▲

Sugar is extracted from the white root, and the pulp and leafy tops fed to livestock. Sugar Beet provides about one third of Britain's sugar.

Lucerne ▲

Grown mainly in south and east England, for animal feed. Grows to 1 m high. Produces purple flowers in June and July.

Kale ▲

Grows to about 1 m. Related to the cabbage. Both the stem and leaves are used for feeding farm animals.

◄ Friesian

Black and white. Produces more milk than other types of cattle, and is also used for beef.

▲ Hereford

Red with a white face. Good for beef.

Jersey ▶

A small cow giving very creamy milk. Has a pale brown coat.

◄ Guernsey

Coat a warmer fawn colour than Jersey, with white patches. Gives very creamy milk.

▲ Cheviot

Seen on hills and mountains. Has hairless white head and no horns.

Blackface ▶

Both rams and ewes have horns. A very hardy sheep found on hills and moors.

◄ Suffolk

Hairless black face. Has no horns. Found all over Britain.

▲ Large White pig

Pale pink all over. Used mainly for bacon.

Saddleback pig ▶

Black with a white band over shoulder. Used for pork and bacon.

Things to look for

In spring

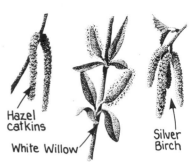

Hazel catkins

White Willow

Silver Birch

▲ The best time to look for flowers of deciduous woodland is in spring. Since the trees are just beginning to grow leaves, there is still enough light on the woodland floor for plants to flower.

▲ Many trees flower in the spring before the leaves are fully grown. Hazel is one of the earliest plants to flower, its catkins turning yellow in February. Willow and Birch catkins open not long after.

House Martin

Green Woodpecker

Song Thrush

▲ Birds are often seen in pairs in spring since this is the time when they find a mate. Many birds sing to attract mates, so the countryside is full of birdsong.

You may see birds' nests later in spring. Be careful not to disturb nesting birds. The House Martin builds a nest of mud and grass under the eaves of houses. The Great Spotted Woodpecker nests in a tree hole. The Song Thrush, like many birds, builds a nest of twigs, grass, moss and mud, usually in a bush or tree.

Cheviot sheep

▲ The lambing season starts in early spring. Newborn lambs can walk within minutes of birth.

In summer

▲ You can find birds' feathers on the ground at any time of the year but early spring and mid-summer are the best times for looking. This is when birds moult, that is shed feathers and grow new ones.

▼ Summer is the time of year when the highest numbers of butterflies are seen on the wing.

Like many insects, butterflies start life as an egg but must pass through other stages of development before becoming adult.

The eggs are laid, usually on a plant. The caterpillar, or larva, hatches out and feeds on the plant until it is fully grown.

It then changes into a pupa, or chrysalis. The adult butterfly develops inside the pupa until it is ready to emerge. It then breaks out of the pupal skin.

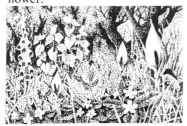

1. Eggs
2. Caterpillar (or larva)

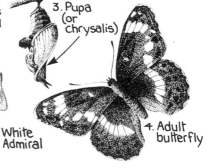

3. Pupa (or chrysalis)
4. Adult butterfly
White Admiral

June and July are rich months for flowers. Look on roadsides, in grassy places and in hedgerows.▼

In the woods, however, the trees in full leaf shade out too much light for many plants to flower.

If you visit heathland or moorland in late summer you will see the pinks and mauves of flowering heather. ▼

In autumn

Swallows gathering on a telegraph wire

▲ You may see flocks of birds gathering, getting ready to migrate, that is to fly back to warmer countries where there are good food supplies in the winter. They will return in the spring.

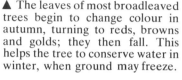

▲ Autumn is the best time to look for mushrooms, toadstools and other fungi. Many kinds of fungi feed on dead plants and animals. They therefore help break down dead material and return nutrients to the soil.

▲ The leaves of most broadleaved trees begin to change colour in autumn, turning to reds, browns and golds; they then fall. This helps the tree to conserve water in winter, when ground may freeze.

▼ See if you can find these fruits and berries in autumn. Blackberries can be eaten and so can Sweet Chestnuts if roasted. You can thread conkers onto string and have conker fights with them.

Plants produce fruits and seeds so that these can be spread around and grow into new plants in new places, away from the parent plant. There are many ways in which the seeds are scattered.

For instance if blackberries are eaten by an animal the seeds will be passed out through its droppings. Many fruits can be carried by wind: for example the Sycamore has a winged fruit and Rosebay Willowherb a fluffy one, so both are easily carried away on the wind. The hooked fruits of Herb Bennet catch onto the coats of passing animals.

Blackberry

Dogrose hips

Sweet Chesnut

Horse Chestnut

Beech nut

(conker)

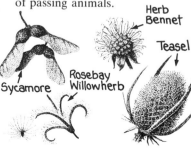

Sycamore

Rosebay Willowherb

Herb Bennet

Teasel

In winter

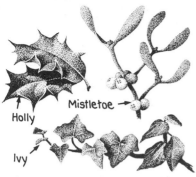

Holly
Mistletoe →
Ivy

▲ Some plants (evergreens) stay green all year: look out for Holly, Ivy and Mistletoe.

▲ Many birds form flocks in winter, and can be seen feeding in fields and woodlands. Insects and berries are scarce in winter, so birds fatten up in autumn to prepare themselves for the lack of food.

Grey Squirrel
Hedgehog (hibernating)

▲ Grey Squirrels may be seen sniffing around on the ground, searching out nuts which they may have buried during the autumn.

The Hedgehog makes a nest under thick vegetation such as Brambles, and hibernates during the cold winter months. It goes into a deep sleep and its temperature drops.

▼ In winter many plants turn brown and wither. Bracken turns rusty-brown. Look for Traveller's Joy which climbs over trees and hedges: its grey downy fruits give the plant its other name – Old Man's Beard.

Bracken is rusty-brown in winter

Old Man's Beard has fluffy fruits

The twigs of broadleaved trees have interesting buds during winter.

▼ Horse Chestnut has stout twigs with sticky brown buds.

▼ Beech has long, pointed, copper-brown buds.

▼ English Oak has clusters of stout light brown buds.

Making a nature diary

Try keeping a diary of changes in the countryside from season to season, as well as anything interesting you see on your walks in the country.

Take a notebook with you for making notes and sketches. If you have a camera, take photographs, especially of the landscape and of trees and other plants.

Keep an album at home for writing up your diary. A looseleaf binder is a good idea since you can add pages whenever you like.

Write the date at the top of each page. You can then make drawings of animals and plants you have seen, or mount photographs, and sellotape in things you have collected such as feathers, and leaves and grasses which you have already pressed and dried between sheets of newspaper. You could record changes you see on farmland, such as ploughing, sowing, harvesting, lambing, as well as those that happen in woods and hedgerows and other habitats.

Help protect the countryside

The Country Code

Protect all wildlife.
Do not pick wild plants, flowers, or break branches from trees. It is illegal to uproot plants other than on your own land or with the owner's permission. Never interfere with any bird's nest or disturb nesting birds.

Guard against all risk of fire.
A burning cigarette or match can start a fire and destroy large areas of countryside, killing the wildlife that lives and grows there.

Close and fasten all gates.
Avoid damaging fences, hedges and walls.
Farm animals straying onto the road may cause accidents, and, if they get into the wrong field, they may destroy the crops growing there.

Do not leave litter.
Litter spoils the countryside for others, and may harm animals if they eat it.

Keep dogs under proper control.
Keep your dog on a lead and do not let it frighten wild birds and mammals or farm animals. A farmer is entitled to shoot dogs seen worrying his animals.

Keep to paths across farmland.
Then you will not risk damaging crops. The same is true in all types of countryside: always try to avoid trampling vegetation needlessly.

Safeguard water supplies
Country streams run into larger rivers which may be used to supply drinking water. Do not pollute the streams with anything, and especially not with oil or other chemicals. Do not put tins or bottles in the water, since these may damage the feet of sheep and cattle drinking at the stream.

Drive carefully on country roads.
Also do not park in narrow lanes or on grass verges, or in front of the entrances to fields.

Respect the life of the countryside.
Leave all wild and cultivated places as you found them.

Glossary

Antenna (plural: antennae) – most insects have a pair of antennae (feelers) which they use for feeling and smelling.

Anthers – the part of a flower which produces the pollen.

Arachnid – a group which includes spiders, ticks and mites. Often thought of as insects but differing in having eight legs, while insects have six.

Breeding season – the time of year when a pair of animals mate and the females give birth and look after their young.

Broadleaved trees – have broad, flat leaves. Most broadleaved trees are deciduous, that is they drop their leaves each autumn.

Conifers – trees with narrow, needle-like or scaly leaves. Most conifers are evergreen, that is the leaves stay on all year. Conifers bear cones.

Creeping (plant) – one of which grows outwards along the ground rather than upwards.

Deciduous (trees) – one which drops its leaves each autumn.

Evergreen – plant which keeps its green leaves all year.

Frond – the leaf-like part of a fern.

Fruit – plants produce fruits containing seeds which are then scattered around so they can grow into new plants.

Habitat – the kind of place in which an animal or plant lives, including the plant life, type of soil and climate of the place.

Larva (plural: larvae) – the form which most insects take after hatching from the egg but before becoming adult, e.g. caterpillar is the larva of a butterfly.

Migration – the regular movement of animals, especially birds, from one area or country to another, usually from the breeding area to the area where they spend the winter. Migrating birds are called **migrants** or **visitors**.

Mollusc – animals, such as snails and mussels, which have a soft body, often protected by an outer shell.

Moult – when animals shed their fur or feathers and grow new ones.

Queen – the large breeding female in a colony of "social insects" such as ants, and some bees and wasps.

Roost – to sleep (birds only). A roost is a place where birds sleep.

Rump – the lower back and base of the tail of a bird.

Rut – the mating period of deer and other hoofed animals.

Seed – see fruit.

Shrub – woody plant which differs from a tree in that it has several woody stems rather than one trunk. Usually smaller than a tree.

Spawn – groups or strings of eggs laid by frogs, toads and fishes.

Species – type of animal, e.g. Black-headed Gull is the name of one species in a group of birds called gulls.

Tadpole – young frog or toad, which lives and swims in water.

Visitor – see migration.

Books to read

General
Family Naturalist. Michael Chinery (Macdonald & Jane's).
Nature Detective. Hugh Falkus (Penguin Books).
On Nature's Trail. Ken Hoy (Mitchell Beazley).
Book of the British Countryside. (AA book published by Drive Publications).

Field guides
For more species to spot, the Spotter's Guides series, published by Usborne, includes titles on Birds, Wild Flowers, Trees, Animals, Butterflies, Insects, Mushrooms. See back cover for information on other titles.

Collins publish the following Field Guides which are small enough to be carried around:
The Birds of Britain and Europe.
The Wild Flowers of Britain and Northern Europe.
The Mammals of Britain and Europe.
The Insects of Britain.

Other good identification guides are *Wild Flowers*, *Trees*, *Grasses*, *Ferns*, *Mosses & Lichens*, and *Mushrooms*, all written by Roger Phillips and published by Pan Books. Also, *British Butterflies*. Robert Goodden (David & Charles).

Useful addresses

If you write for information to any of the organizations listed here, please remember to enclose a *stamped, self-addressed envelope* for your reply.

The Nature Conservancy Council publishes wallcharts, posters and books on wildlife and conservation. Their catalogue is available free from: Interpretative Branch, Nature Conservancy Council, Attingham Park, Shrewsbury SY4 4TW. Your envelope should be at least 20 cm x 21 cm.

The Royal Society for the Protection of Birds (RSPB), The Lodge, Sandy, Beds, is the national society for anyone interested in birds. The Young Ornithologists' Club (Y.O.C.) is the junior section for people 15 years old and under.

You can get the address of your local **County Naturalists' Trust** from the Royal Society for Nature Conservation, 22 The Green, Nettleham, Lincoln LN2 2NR. They will also give you information about the **WATCH** club – the junior branch of the Nature Conservation Trusts. **WATCH** has its own magazine, special projects and local groups in all areas.

You can find out the address of your local **Natural History Society** from CoEnCo, Zoological Gardens, Regents Park, London NW1.

Scorecard

The species are in alphabetical order. When you go out spotting, put the date at the top of a blank column and, in the same column, fill in the score for each species you see. At the end of the day, put your total score at the foot of each page. Then add up your grand total.

Species	Score	Date	Date	Date	Species	Score	Date	Date	Date
Admiral, Red	10				Buttercup, Creeping	5			
Agaric, Fly	15				Campion, Red	10			
Ant, Red	5				Carrot, Wild	10			
Ash, Common	5				Celandine, Lesser	5			
Barley	5				Chaffinch	5			
Beech, Common	5				Chestnut, Horse	5			
Beetle, Violet Ground	5				Chestnut, Sweet	5			
Beet, Sugar	5				Cinquefoil, Creeping	5			
Bindweed, Greater	5				Clover, White	5			
Birch, Silver	5				Coot	10			
Blackberry	5				Coriolus versicolor	5			
Blackbird	5				Crow, Carrion	5			
Blue, Common	5				Daddy Long Legs	5			
Bluebell	10				Daisy	5			
Bracken	5				Daisy, Ox-eye	10			
Brimstone	15				Damselfly, Blue-tailed	10			
Brown, Meadow	5				Dandelion	5			
Bullfinch	10				Dead-nettle, White	10			
Bumblebee, Buff-tailed	5				Deer, Fallow	15			
Burnet, Six-spot	10				Deer, Roe	15			
Bush Cricket, Speckled	10				Dogrose	10			
Buttercup, Bulbous	5				Dove, Collared	10			
Total					Total				

Species	Score	Date	Date	Date	Species	Score	Date	Date	Date
Dragonfly, Golden-ringed	10				Heather	5			
Dunnock	5				Hedgehog	10			
Earwig, Common	5				Herb Bennet,	10			
Elder	5				Herb Robert	10			
Fir, Douglas	10				Hereford cattle	5			
Fox, Red	15				Heron, Grey	10			
Foxglove	10				Holly	5			
Friesian cattle	5				Honeysuckle	5			
Frog, Common	10				Ink Cap, Shaggy	5			
Goldfinch	10				Ivy	5			
Goosegrass	5				Jack-by-the-Hedge	5			
Gorse	10				Jay	10			
Grass, Common Couch	5				Jersey cattle	10			
Grass, Common Cocksfoot	5				Kale	10			
Grass, Common Reed	10				Kestrel	10			
Grass, Red Fescue	5				Knapweed	10			
Grass, Timothy	5				Lady's Smock	10			
Grass, Yorkshire Fog	10				Ladybird, Seven-spot	5			
Greenfinch	10				Lapwing	10			
Groundsel	5				Lucerne	10			
Guernsey cattle	10				Magpie	10			
Gull, Black-headed	5				Mallard	5			
Hawthorn	5				Meadowsweet	10			
Heath, Small	5				Moorhen	5			
Total					Total				

Species	Score	Date	Date	Date	Species	Score	Date	Date	Date
Mouse, Wood	10				Ragwort	5			
Mustard	10				Rape	5			
Nettle	5				Rape, Oil-seed	10			
Nightshade, Black	10				Reed, Common	10			
Nightshade, Woody	10				Reedmace, Lesser	10			
Oak, English	5				Robin	5			
Oak, Sessile	5				Rook	10			
Oats	10				Rowan	10			
Old Man's Beard	10				Rush, Soft	5			
Painted Lady	15				Scabious, Devil's Bit	10			
Parasol	10				Scabious, Field	10			
Parsley, Cow	5				Sheep, Blackface	5			
Peacock	10				Sheep, Cheviot	10			
Pheasant	5				Sheep, Suffolk	5			
Pig, Large White	5				Shrew, Common	10			
Pig, Saddleback	10				Silverweed	10			
Pimpernel, Scarlet	10				Snake, Grass	15			
Pine, Scots	10				Snail, Garden	5			
Plantain, Greater	5				Sorrel, Wood	5			
Poplar, Lombardy	10				Sparrow, House	5			
Poppy	5				Speedwell, Common	10			
Primrose	10				Spider, Garden	5			
Rabbit	5				Squirrel, Grey	5			
Ragged Robin	10				Starling	5			
Total					Total				

Species	Score	Date	Date	Date	Species	Score	Date	Date	Date
Stitchwort, Greater	5				Tufted Duck	10			
Stoat	15				Vetch, Tufted	10			
Sulphur Tuft	10				Violet, Common Dog	10			
Swallow	10				Vole, Field	10			
Swan, Mute	10				Wagtail, Pied	10			
Swift	10				Wasp, Common	5			
Sycamore	5				Weasel	15			
Thrush, Song	5				Wheat	5			
Tiger Moth, Garden	10				White, Large	5			
Tit, Blue	5				Willowherb, Rosebay	5			
Tit, Coal	10				Woodpecker, Great Spotted	15			
Tit, Great	5				Woodpigeon	5			
Toad, Common	10				Woundwort, Wood	10			
Tortoiseshell, Small	5				Wren	10			
Trefoil, Birds's Foot	10				Yarrow	5			
Total					Total				
					Grand Total				

Index

63